THE
RUBBER BAND
RESILIENT
LEADER

How to Stretch
Without Snapping

KATHY *Parry*

Corporate Energy Expert

The
Rubber-Band-Resilient Leader

How to Stretch Without Snapping

Printed in the United States of America

ISBN: 9781096429623

Credits:

Copy Editor	Kathleen Green, Positively Proofed, Plano, TX, info@positivelyproofed.com
Design, art direction, and production	Melissa Farr, Back Porch Creative, Frisco, TX, info@BackPorchCreative.com

Dedication

My previous three books were all dedicated to people I love: my children, parents and family. But this book felt different, and it became clear whom I needed to dedicate it to.

This book is dedicated to different versions of me because Kathy Parry today couldn't have written this without these other Kathy Parrys:

Ten-year-old Kathy Parry, who thought she could do almost anything;

Thirty-seven-year-old Kathy Parry, who stretched and almost snapped;

Forty-six-year-old Kathy Parry, who remembered she could do almost anything and snapped back.

Read This First

Are you feeling stretched? Is it your job, your co-workers, your kids, your finances? The list is endless. Imagine your life as a pile of rubber bands representing all of your stresses. Would each band be stretched to the breaking point? *The Rubber-Band-Resilient Leader* gives you the inspiration and information you need to finally maneuver through transitional events without snapping.

Whether your organization is going through a restructuring, your team has been charged with increasing productivity or you need to manage your aging father's medical issues while balancing your own family's schedule, the tips, stories and tools in the pages ahead will make the disruptions easier.

Each chapter tells a bit about my resilience journey and takes an inspirational look at other resilient professionals. At the end of each chapter, you will find "Tips, Tools and Tactics." Take time to really go through these exercises. Have a notebook handy. If you're reading this with a group or team, work through the questions together. (Consider inviting me to facilitate a meeting!)

I wrote this book because I experienced the stretch, and I almost snapped. Instead, I used the methods in this book to snap back and re-energize from the biggest stretch of my life.

Go get your notebook and a big rubber band. Turn the page and get ready to become rubber-band resilient.

Table of Contents

Introduction

What do you do when you get the most devastating news of your life? Real-life scenarios such as these have the potential to turn your professional and personal life upside down:

- Your division is moving to St. Louis, but your children are heavily entrenched in high school sports and have no desire to go anywhere.

- The third-quarter-earnings downturn is a direct result of a plan you implemented. The higher-ups are murmuring about possible layoffs.

- A key team member leading your company's largest client project is diagnosed with a debilitating disease.

Such devastating news is certainly within the realm of real possibilities. How would any one of these worst-case scenarios affect your ability to lead? What would be your next move?

When I started working with organizations, leading workshops and delivering keynotes about resilient behaviors, I had to take a deep introspective look at my own life. In order to be the authority in the room, I needed reassurance that I was able to overcome one of the most difficult obstacles someone could face … without snapping.

Oftentimes when I got up in front of several hundred leaders, I wondered, "Are they asking, 'Who is this woman? Her bio says nothing about leading a multimillion- or billion-dollar company.'" I know that *all* leaders need to understand resiliency, not just managers, sales professionals or C-suite executives. Even worried moms sitting in hospital rooms need tenacious coping skills. I know. I've been there.

In a dimly lit exam room, I watched as electrodes were removed from my 12-week-old daughter's head. Small flakes of glue peppered her baby hospital gown. I didn't care about the mess. I just wanted her in my arms.

Earlier that week I had noticed some unusual movements coming from my fourth child. She jerked a bit in a repetitive manner and then smiled. At first, I thought it was cute, but then I got worried. Her pediatrician sent us to UPMC Children's Hospital of Pittsburgh for further examination.

The pediatric neurologist entered the room as I picked the glue off Merritt's head, like a mama monkey attending to her young. "I'm sorry to tell you this, but the EEG showed signs of seizure activity."

Seizure activity. What? What did that mean? Was she having a seizure right then? Was she going to keep having seizures? I needed some answers. My thoughts had already started drifting toward the sitter at home tending to my three "older" children – six, four and two years old. In the face of adversity, I was already thinking about my young charges.

One day in the hospital turned into a week of tests and tears. It also turned into a crisis-management situation. With four young children, I was a full-blown, 24/7 manager of lives. I wasn't at the helm of a multimillion-dollar company but rather entrusted with life's most precious commodities. This CEO was falling apart fast.

Six months later, I got even more devastating news. Merritt's seizures were a sign of a metabolic disease. Her cells did not properly turn food into energy. She slept 20 hours a day and wasn't developing, and I struggled to get food into her. The doctor grimly stated, "We can't really expect her to live more than two years."

What happens when you hear devastating news like this? First, you react. After that initial reaction, which is often visceral and raw, you get to decide:

How will this define me?

What can I do to change the outcome?

Who will I inspire or how will I affect others with my actions?

Leading under adverse conditions can happen in conference rooms or playrooms. It is not the sight of the adversity but the subsequent reactions – reframing of the issue and re-energizing of your soul – that turn you into a rubber-band-resilient leader. Can you stretch without snapping?

At the end of each section, you will have the opportunity to explore how you can personally address that phase of resilience. Do these exercises. Write them down. Take them to your team meeting. Better yet, work through this book with your team. Understanding how those around you handle disruptions creates a more cohesive, engaged and productive organization.

In this book, I will share stories of resilient leaders – those who faced a myriad of crises, predicaments, emergencies and basic run-of-the-mill disasters. These leaders' commonalities determine their success once they've reached the other side of their tragic or debilitating event.

I know. The greatest crisis of my life made me an expert in resiliency.

chapter one

What's Stretching You?

That first year of a devastating diagnosis with my daughter Merritt stretched me to my snapping point many times. A crisis has a life and, in its infancy, a crisis is all about reaction. Anger, grief, lack of control and anxiety are just a few of the emotions that cry out. The next three chapters offer more insight into how to march through the reaction phase. I was a newbie in the crisis world, so I wasn't sure how to get through this first phase. Life had gone pretty much according to plan until my daughter was diagnosed. One day while grappling with my initial reactions, I remembered the first time I understood that others go through events such as these that cause their world to slow.

In 1978, I stood in my father's office as he proudly hung a new piece of artwork on his wall. My mother and I had driven to downtown Akron, Ohio, to hand-deliver this installation. Earlier that day, we had picked up the art from the frame shop. My mother was so excited to get this to my father, so we dropped everything and headed into town.

As we unwrapped the brown craft paper from the frame, I watched my father's signature grin spread across his face. His family nickname was "The Grinch," not because his heart was too small but just the opposite – my father was a man with the biggest heart I knew. He would hire immigrants with no other means for making money, give endless hours to raise money for organizations like the Salvation Army and YMCA and cry with me when a car hit my favorite cat. My father was "The Grinch" because the man had a toothy grin that literally lit up his face like when the Grinch of the Christmas story discovered he could help the Whos down in Whoville. My father was a helper, a do-gooder, a happy soul.

So I was baffled as he hung his new office art and explained the meaning. Hanging in an impressive frame were Chinese symbols. A family friend had spent time studying in China, a bit of a progressive place to be in the 1970s, before the explosion in our global economy. When my mother found out she could get an authentic rendering of one of my father's favorite sayings, she commissioned a family friend to make it happen.

"It means 'crisis,'" my father explained as he stepped back a few feet to admire the new piece. The two symbols that made up the piece seemed to flow with a swiftness that represented something less ominous than "crisis." "The top symbol means 'danger' and the bottom symbol stands for 'opportunity,'" he continued. "Do you understand that?"

I was 14. I understood hairstyles, eighth-grade boy drama and how to bake really good cookies. My world did not yet include crises or danger, unless it was in the form of riding on the back of my neighbor's moped with no helmet.

"I get that a crisis can be dangerous, but how is a crisis an opportunity?" I asked. The Grinchy grin faded just a bit and he said, "Well, when you have something happen that isn't what you expected, you can face danger, but it is also the time to make changes happen. And often those changes are better than what would have happened before the crisis. Opportunities that you never would have even thought about may now present themselves."

I pondered my father's words as we headed home. Crisis? What crisis did he ever have? He ran a business that his grandfather started. From a small welding shop, the business had grown under his father's leadership to a larger operation employing about 50 people. In my world, all seemed smooth when looking at my father. We lived a comfortable lifestyle, not flashy or extravagant, but never feeling like we didn't have what we needed. He golfed, worked on our five acres producing a wonderful bounty from his garden and he laughed often, especially when chiding my mother or asking for another piece of pie.

Years later, though, I began to understand the meaning and significance of my father's crisis.

His father, the leader of the company and patriarch of a large family, had passed away very suddenly two years before. I was sad to lose my grandfather, but I had absolutely no understanding what that had done to my father. At age 42, the eldest of seven siblings, he stepped into the role of running a company and a family. This event stretched my father nearly to his breaking point.

When I speak to organizations about resilience, I use the example of a rubber band to explain the potential found in disruption.

Picture a loose, lonely rubber band sitting on your desk. It is doing nothing. Just sitting. If you picked it up and did not stretch it but rather just let go of it, it would drop limply to your desk. Now, if you picked up that same rubber band and pulled it back as far as you felt comfortable doing so (don't snap it on your fingers!), you know it will shoot far. Go ahead: Picture it. Better yet, pick up a rubber band right now. Aim it at the ceiling, not your co-worker, and let it go. It hit the ceiling, right?!

A stretched rubber band can fly across the room. Remember back to ninth-grade science class and how the energy contained in that stretched rubber band was called potential energy. When the rubber band is not stretched, it flops to the ground. No potential energy.

But pull back, get a bit uncomfortable and, BAM, that thing will fly.

Your disruption, crisis or change is the stretch. Its energy has potential for greatness.

My father was stretched when he had to suddenly run a company. I was stretched when I found out I would have a new role as a mother of a handicapped child. Your stretch may be personal or professional. To become more resilient during events that stretch us, we must first identify the events. Sometimes we know they're coming, like new technology or a regulation that we must employ. Other times, a security breach involving your clients' data or a burst water main that floods your office takes you completely off-guard.

Stress, confusion and fear, my father told me years later, were all a part of his reaction to his new reality. These are often the feelings we think about when we are faced with a crisis. In the next three chapters, we're going to examine how leaders, faced with disruption, reacted in such a way that helped frame their situation.

Reaction, whether to an individual or organizational crisis, is the starting point in how we create opportunity out of the situation. The appropriate reactions, both at the beginning of an event and through its lifetime, are what separate great leaders from those who dwell in pity and blame others.

Reactions come in several forms. There are seven general reactions to grief. We don't just grieve over the loss of a loved one. We grieve over the loss of a client, a job or a contract. The early, initial reactions, like the one I experienced when the doctor told me my daughter would only live a couple of years, are visceral and raw, gut-wrenching pain and shock. When my father lost his father, he started with pain and shock.

The next set of reactions comes when you decide to move forward, an upward turn in thinking. You begin to move on from the danger of the crisis and begin looking for the opportunity.

At every step in the reacting process, a resilient leader should keep opportunity in mind. It isn't always easy to see in the dark hours, but this knowledge can propel you through the grieving process.

As my father's new reality set in, he knew that in order to be resilient and continue to lead the company, he needed to stay focused on the opportunities that surely would come. In the next 20 years, he grew the business to more than 300 employees, buying other smaller distributors along the way. He later reflected that if his father had not left the helm of the company so suddenly, they would have puttered along at a pace that my grandfather was more comfortable with. Without his father there to hold him back, my father steered the company to new opportunities.

Reactions are hard to control, and they happen all day long. You may be reacting to a person, an event or even standstill traffic on the way to a client. Understanding that while you may not have one speck of control over the situation, you can really only control your own reaction.

The first phase of becoming more rubber-band resilient is to understand the stretch. What is stretching you? How are you reacting to the stretch? Get a big rubber band and let's work out your disruption together through the exercises in this book.

Tips, Tools and Tactics
to Understand Your Reactions

1. What are you reacting to today?

2. Where are your crises? Are they truly crises? Are you giving them too much reaction? Not enough reaction?

3. How do your reactions affect your team?

4. Is there someone in your organization whose reactions are inappropriate? Have they been addressed?

chapter two

Honor Initial Reactions

I ate pizza. Not a little pizza – a lot of pizza. And wine. Many glasses of wine. Then I got on the phone. I called my parents, my siblings and my friends. I needed to hear those words – words that were consumed like the pizza and wine that maybe, just maybe, numbed what I was feeling.

That was my reaction the night I learned my daughter had one of the worst possible diseases in the spectrum of mitochondrial dysfunctions.

I am betting that many of you have had similar reactions. After the shock, pain is the second feeling we generally have when faced with a crisis. We try to ease that pain with food, alcohol, shopping, drugs or other destructive methods.

Was it self-pity? Maybe a little. Many of us want someone to understand our pain when the disruptive event happens. Maybe you're a stoic. You don't show pain. No reaction. Well, that is a reaction, too.

The moment after you receive the news, your initial reactions are the most raw. Those first reactions are what you feel when a car rear-ends your car, your house is going up in flames or your stock portfolio plummets.

Your brain doesn't go to what's next. Your body just reacts.

I sat on my deck outside until about 9 p.m. despite knowing I needed to get inside and put the older children to bed. With a tear-streaked face, I had to move on. My initial reaction was pain and sadness. Instead, I embraced it. I didn't know what was next, but I forced myself to stop the pain for awhile and put on a false attitude of hope as I tucked my children into bed.

What is important about the initial reaction for resilient people? It's understanding your go-to reaction. Yep. It isn't really a hard step in the process to becoming more resilient or building more resilient teams. The first moments of a disruption are unpredictable, so we can't really predict how we'll feel. In this stage of a disruptive event, it is important just to honor your initial reaction. In saying that, it then becomes important to honor everyone else's first reactions.

So how do you do that? Spend some time observing how individuals on your team react. Don't comment on their reactions. Just notice. If you hear dramatic sighs from Julie every time you mention the new software system, take note. Or if Phil needs to interrupt others in a strategy session to make his point, take note. We generally react to the bigger disruptions with a more emphasized version of our daily reactions. If a major event happens, such as a merger or an announcement about downsizing, you can bet Phil is going to make sure his point is heard very loudly, and Julie is going to stir up some drama. As the stakes rise, emotions can become more intense. Study the reactions of those around you and see how they process events. When you understand how others react to change, you can better navigate positive communication, ultimately managing the event in order to reach a positive outcome.

It is equally important to understand that initial reactions (while the most emotional) will most likely not last the duration of the event. After my daughter's diagnosis, I didn't eat and drink my way through the next year. (Although I did make double-dark chocolate brownies more often.) I learned to honor those initial reactions for what they were – pure emotion to an uncertain event. By honoring this, I was able to move through next steps.

A Flood of Reactions

Dan's business success story is one of my favorites. Motivated by a need to be on his own and a desire to prove he had what it took to be an entrepreneur, Dan launched his own custom packaging business in 1997 in Pittsburgh. He saw a need and created a product to get industrial steel wrapped and ready for transport. His gregarious personality makes him a natural salesperson, but other aspects of growing a business challenged him. In 2001, one of his biggest customers filed for bankruptcy, leaving Dan and his bank account high and dry. This was his first major setback and nearly cost him his business. In September 2004, a second devastating disruption happened.

When Hurricane Ivan, a Category 3 swirl of destruction, left the Gulf Coast, its remnants dumped six inches of rain on Pittsburgh in less than 24 hours. Dan's facility was located near a small creek that had never been declared a flood zone … until that September day. Dan and his employees were forced to evacuate as the creek rose quickly, cutting off roadways and stranding people. When Dan was able to get back to his two buildings, he "witnessed a complete nightmare" and dropped to his knees. Dan saw firsthand how quickly 33 inches of rushing water could decimate a business. Everything on the production floor was a 100 percent loss and the electrical system was waterlogged. When he opened his file cabinet drawers, muddy water drained out.

Dan's initial reaction was despair. Remember that he had just faced a major hit to his fledgling business a few years before this event. "I wanted to just throw my hands in the air, walk away, go home, get drunk and feel sorry for myself," Dan recalled. But those initial reactions were short-lived. "I only gave myself a couple of hours, tops," Dan recalls. "I quickly realized that this is not what I am made of. I will survive this. I had to survive this. My family, my employees and my loyal vendors are all counting on me. This process was exhausting and long and required a lot of 'positive acting,' but after 10 days, the loss of 15 pounds and no sleep, we were cleaned up and off and running."

As Dan recounted these events, he realized that keeping his emotions from the initial reaction bottled up probably left more of a scar than he realized. He was in survival mode after initially feeling despair. In the years after the flood, Dan has been able to honor those initial reactions, realizing that his fears help fuel his success.

Tips, Tools and Tactics
to Embrace the Initial Reaction

1. Think of a time when you heard bad news. How did you react in the first few hours? What actions did you take in that first hour? Make a list of the feelings you experienced.

2. Did anyone else see you react?

3. Did this specific event change the way you react to other disruptions?

chapter three

React –
Not All Reactions Are the Same

When I was dealing with my daughter's diagnosis, I had to talk about it. A lot. It helped me. My reaction included reaching out, sharing my grief and gathering energy from others. My ex-husband? Not so much. He didn't want to talk about it. He needed to internalize the situation. That was his method of dealing. I remember a conversation that ended with him saying, "You can't tell me how to feel."

He was right.

We desperately want others to feel what we're feeling when we are faced with disruptions. A friend, when faced with a huge project, recently said, "Why don't they understand how this project is affecting me? Don't they get that I now need to work later, skip my workout, and pay extra for childcare?"

"No," I told her, "they may not get that."

Everyone has different reactions, but to create smooth transitions through disruptive events, we must honor those reactions – not judge, not create drama.

We run into trouble when different reactions collide. We can get a hot mess of feelings and drama and blame … oh, my. When people react to the same disruption without understanding how others process, it has the potential for a meltdown.

These meltdowns present themselves in a couple of ways. First is projection. When someone can't deal with their own emotions, they often project onto another person. This is some Psychology 101 stuff. If you don't face what you're feeling because it is uncomfortable, then it may be easier to pass those feelings on to someone else. For example, Joe is unsettled by the announcement of a department restructuring. He fears for his job because the new manager may not understand how he processes information. Instead of admitting his fear and asking his new manager how they can make this work, Joe begins to lash out at individuals who are new to the department. He creates drama and incivility among his team by placing blame elsewhere.

Owning emotions is the best way to stop projection. Managers need to help their team understand why it is OK to show emotion and help them process what they're feeling. This takes us to the second type of trouble: communicating the emotion on a professional level.

Have you ever cried at work? I have. My first job out of college was with a super-regional bank in the South. As a 22-year-old in a professional setting, I didn't have all of the coping skills I needed. I didn't fully understand how to deal with my middle-aged male manager. One day I just needed to cry. But how? Where? Luckily, I had an assistant manager who totally understood what I needed: an ear. I needed to vent and be heard. Fortunately, I found the right person, in a closed office. We worked through my emotions together in less than 15 minutes and all was well in branch operations.

We've seen some really unfortunate examples of employees who didn't feel heard. An actual phrase has been added to our slang vocabulary based on disgruntled employees who lack an outlet for expressing their feelings at work. "Going postal" is no joke as it refers to shootings at U.S. Postal Service facilities by employees who probably had no outlet for their reactions to an event at work.

Understanding your own way of reacting to situations is the first part of creating a strong team. The second, though, is coming to an understanding of those around you. Not everyone is a worst-case-scenario person. But if one person on a team is, and they are constantly told that their reaction is not appropriate, they will begin to feel defensive or of no value to the organization. Honoring everyone's initial reaction is the second phase of reacting. In order to stay resilient during the reaction stage, all reactions must be honored. This phase is still highly personal. The team will come together during the reframing stage but, for now, it's best to react and honor all reactions.

Tony Didn't Honor Reactions

Sherry was a vice president at a large pharmaceutical company. She led a project team with Tony, another vice president. Together they were leading a team to complete a huge project with a tight deadline. The head of the division called Sherry and Tony in for a late-afternoon meeting. He broke the news that they would need to put in extra hours, including evenings. Sherry was visibly upset and started shuffling papers and sighing. Tony took advantage of Sherry's reaction, and not in a positive way.

Tony thought this was a great opportunity to show off his skills and get more attention from the higher-ups. He knew Sherry had young children. Looking over at Sherry in the meeting, he said, "Do you have childcare issues, Sherry?" She was seething. Tony had undermined her with this comment. Tension prevailed as Sherry tried to defend herself in front of the manager. However, when longer hours were mentioned, she had been dramatic. Tony did not build up his teammate but rather took advantage of her reaction. Sherry continued the project with a lot of animosity toward her co-leader, which is never a great dynamic for project work.

Tips, Tools and Tactics
to Honor Reactions

1. What is your typical reaction to disruptive events? Some of these may include worst-case-scenario thinking, anger, frustration, calm, immediate problem solving, sadness, loss of confidence and/or gossip.

2. Can you predict how people on your team typically react to the same type of events? Jot those reactions down.

3. Are there times when others' reactions make you frustrated, angry or unproductive? How could you better anticipate their reactions and your reaction?

4. If you know that a disruption is coming your way, either personally or professionally, plan a meeting with the team members who will be most affected. Use the exercise provided at www.KathyParry.com/ rubberbandresilience to anticipate reactions and create a smoother transition.

chapter four

Power in the Pause

When I was in the throes of dealing with my daughter's condition, I walked. All. The. Time. When I walked out the door, I felt peace coming back into my life. I wasn't searching the internet for cures. I wasn't talking to doctors or therapists. I wasn't planning her next meal. I was quiet and carving out time to pause. My pauses came on a walking trail near my home. In these moments, I took my stretched life and just let it be still. I had a lot of energy to devote to my family, but I had to keep the power until I knew exactly where and when to unleash it.

The next stage in the reacting phase of a disruption is pausing. If every reaction is immediate, we lose power quickly. When faced with a situation that causes a reaction, it is fine and really OK to just say, "I need some time to think about this" … and be still. Your reaction does not need to create your next action.

Social media does not induce the concept of the pause. The constant connection we have with the world has allowed us to immediately share our reaction with millions of others. Instead of going to the woods for a quiet, mind-clearing walk, we Tweet about bad service at the new restaurant, throw our family under the bus with a post about an ex-in-law or share the injustice of a political foe. This isn't the overreacting I'm talking about. Instead, it's reacting too quickly.

Pauses make us uncomfortable. We get antsy when things aren't immediate in our instant-information society. Do you go crazy when you lose cell service? Is it maddening when you're put on hold for too long when calling the cable company?

When I was in grade school, my parents bought us an Encyclopaedia Britannica set. The smell of the freshly printed pages and feel of the stately bound books inspired awe in my 12-year-old brain. I could not wait for the next book report assignment so that I could begin researching. Besides using these books for schoolwork, I would sneak quietly into the living room and randomly grab a heavy leather-bound book off the shelf and sit for hours looking over facts. My kids wonder why I'm so good at Jeopardy. I don't think I'm that smart. I wouldn't consider myself worthy of being a Jeopardy contestant. I do think a number of random facts from those pages stuck in the crevices of my brain. My study of the set took time. It was how I expected to learn.

Now we have Wikipedia and the entire world of knowledge in our smartphones. We are accustomed to instantaneous information. Unfortunately, this impatience transfers to our daily lives. When disruptions cause us to react, we may not have all of the information we need to take the next step. We don't know what the MRI will reveal or how the failed test run of the new operating system will affect our time line or if the new regulation will affect our bottom line. We may need to further investigate.

Just because you can make a next move doesn't mean you should. If you are reacting to a situation and it is early in the disruption, go ahead and pause. Taking a next step out of haste can worsen the situation. Words that you can't take back may be said, critical errors that affect others can happen and bottom lines can be affected.

Remember the stretched rubber band? It is at its fullest potential just before you shoot it. The power is in the pause.

If you're feeling that stretch and are not sure how to react, or if you're afraid your reaction may not be the right one, pause. Hold onto that energy for when you know exactly what you want to do.

Social Media's Big Pause

Social media allows instant reactions – no pause. A thought enters your mind; it then becomes a Tweet, a live Facebook video or an Instagram story. We have become so used to the immediate nature of our world that we are shocked by pauses. Many of my friends have posted random quiz results on their Facebook pages. I was always leery of taking these quizzes, even though I certainly wanted to know what fairy princess I was. By checking a box, data gurus behind the quiz would be able to access my account, so I skipped the quizzes.

In early 2018, millions of Americans woke up to learn that their personal data had been harvested from their Facebook accounts. Cambridge Analytica, a research firm, was using data collected off Facebook profiles to help its clients create and target their ads. Some were politically motivated. This breach was a pivotal moment when we began to understand "personal data" and how we were being used.

Facebook's response the day the news broke? Nothing. I woke up and looked for the face of Facebook, CEO Mark Zuckerberg, to have a microphone in his face. Nothing. Day two and the news about the breach started with, "No response from Zuckerberg." This went on for five days. Facebook had nothing to say.

The pause was audible. The pause made us think and conjecture. The pause held a lot of power.

After five days, Facebook sent COO Sheryl Sandberg out to talk. She hit all the major news shows. All of the reporters asked the same first question, "Where have you been the last five days?" Toeing the Zuckerberg line, she responded, "We spent the last few days trying to get to the bottom of it."

Not all responses need to be immediate. Was Facebook in the wrong? Sure, but I was moved by the method they used. In the age of immediacy, pausing allows us to respond with a more measured approach than what we may have offered if we were reacting with emotion.

Tips, Tools and Tactics
for Pausing

1. Do you or your organization use social media to express reactions? How could you use this medium to represent disruptions in a positive way?

2. At your next strategy session, instead of asking for immediate brainstorming ideas, ask your team to pause. Give it a specific time frame of 24 or 48 hours, even a week. Hold the next meeting offsite.

3. Keep a large rubber band on your desk. When you feel the stress of an event, stretch it. As much as you are tempted, do not shoot it … even for fun. Hold that stretch and imagine the potential energy.

chapter five

Reframe the Situation

Did you pick up that rubber band yet and stretch it? When we stretch a rubber band, I'd bet that at least 90 percent of us pulling on that thin piece of elastic are thinking, "I don't want this thing to snap." We hate the surprise snap.

I make smoothies in the morning. Frozen mango is my favorite ingredient, which must go in the smoothie to make it thick and tropical tasting. In the middle of winter in Pittsburgh, I want a tropical taste! I was always stretching a rubber band around the bag of frozen mango and throwing it back in the freezer. The problem was that the bands turned brittle from the constant temperature changes. I was always snapping rubber bands on my hands. It hurt. I got smart and put the mango in a plastic bag. Even now, I always think of that snap when I'm stretching a rubber band.

Chances are that when you're stretched, you feel like you might snap. After we honor the stretch, we have to reframe our situation, so we become more rubber-band resilient and don't snap. We need to snap back. To further understand how this works, let's take a trip to camp.

One of the greatest joys of being a parent has always been summer break – the lack of a schedule, interesting outings and more time with the kids. I waited all year for these magical days … until it got old. I had to reconfigure things to recapture the joy. The answer? Sleepaway camp! I was blessed to find a great camp that my kids loved, and so did I.

My No. 3 kiddo, Graham, unfortunately had to watch his sister go off and have fun at camp and then his brother. Poor Graham would mope around the house for two weeks, missing his siblings and wondering what he was missing at camp. "Mommmm, when do I get to go to camp?" he protested. "Bud, you're only five. You have to wait until after second grade," I told him, much to his dismay.

When Graham finally went to camp, I was anxious to pick him up. Did it live up to his expectations? It sure did. On the way home, Graham was his typical animated self, telling stories of his camp adventures. "I learned how to get in and out of a canoe in the water, and I did the zip line and went to adventure camp overnight," he continued, almost breathless to rehash every event. I'd been down this road before, so I knew I could use the camp experience to my advantage.

"Graham, what did you do after breakfast but before activity time?" I asked, fishing for the answer that would make my life easier.

"Umm, well, we brushed our teeth. And, oh, we did devotions," he remembered.

This wasn't what I was going for. "What about right before you left the cabin?" I prodded.

He looked puzzled. I finally put it out there, "Didn't you HAVE to clean the cabin before you got to do activities?" Obviously I wanted this bit of camp activity to spill over into our daily routine at home.

"Oh, Mom, we didn't HAVE to clean the cabin, we GOT to clean the cabin," he said, blue eyes glinting.

Those counselors played the ninja mind trick we all need when we're trying to reframe any disruptive event. Reframing how we look at things means changing "HAVE TO" to "GOT TO."

This also applies at work. When you're told your team needs to send 75 percent of its members for four days of new compliance training, can you positively reframe that disruption? What if your quarterly numbers are down by 20 percent? How do you change your mindset after your initial reaction?

Well, you stop – even if it's on the side of the road – and ask yourself a few questions.

When my daughter was barely a year old, I knew what was on my plate. I was told that Merritt might only live until age two. If she did live longer, she would be severely disabled. It took me a long time to work through that. I'd obviously been reacting to the news for a while, but what was next? I had a pretty charmed life up until that point. If things went wrong, I always had confidence in my ability, my family and my faith to help me manage. Jobs had come easily, my other children were awesome and I had wonderful friends. But this precious child was challenging everything I had ever known.

One day, while driving, I started crying. The gravity of my situation weighed heavily. All of my normal resources that usually helped reduce the stretch I was feeling were not working that day. I was sad and ready to snap. I pulled the car over. I heard myself saying, "I'm afraid to be the mother of a handicapped child." Wow.

As soon as I said it, I felt the stretch loosen. I went a bit further and asked myself, "What are you so afraid of?" When that small voice in my head got brave enough to answer the question, I heard myself say, "I'm afraid of being sad." I was an optimistic, upbeat person. A friend once said, "How can you be happy all the time?" With Merritt, I had been sad. When people saw me at Starbucks, they gave me "sad eyes." I was afraid that this was the new me.

I had admitted my fear, my big fear. Once I identified my fear, the stretch loosened even further. Maybe I wouldn't snap. After that, I started looking at my life differently. I didn't have to be the mother of a handicapped child; I GOT to be her mother.

That's when new outlets opened. I helped other parents manage their emotions after diagnosis. I pursued a certification in plant-based nutrition to help Merritt, and eventually many others. I decided not to snap. A big part of this happened because I was honest about what I was feeling. I asked myself the hard questions.

Fear is the thing that can make us snap. Fear is just our loss in our confidence as to whether we have the ability to handle a situation.

We can find what we need to reduce the fear and to regain confidence in our abilities. We can stretch without snapping when we reframe our situation.

When we begin to reframe our disruption, good stuff starts to happen. To get through this process, there are some critical steps we must take: allow time to absorb, get creative and build muscle. We'll take a look at these steps in the next three chapters.

Reframing in a Jail Cell

Joseph Gonzales understood fear. Joe was involved in an incident with friends in 1998 that ended in a shooting death. Even though Joe didn't pull the trigger, a man died. Joe was convicted of third-degree murder. He spent the first couple of years of his incarceration feeling hopeless and negative. His life had been on a downward spiral in the years before the tragic event. After serving two years of his 30-year sentence, Joe had a pivotal moment. "After I was transferred to the state penitentiary, I looked in the mirror and said, 'I can continue on this path, or I can start on a new one, now.'" That revelation moved him away from fear and he began to reframe his disrupted life.

Joe decided to use his time to become more educated. He read, studied and applied for many different certifications. Although he began using his time in a constructive way, he said it was his second act of re-framing that made all the difference. Despite having some skills he could use if he were released from prison, he realized he was still thinking in the same way. "I was uncomfortable and realized I had only done half the work. The education was outward work. I had to do some inward work – self-work." This is when he began to read works by others who had suffered adversity. He worked on his mindset. When Joe started saying, "I GET to be in prison," he refined his core principles. This allowed him to change his life and how he viewed the world.

Joe is currently a professional speaker, success trainer and TEDx talk speaker. For more information, visit www.josephjgonzales.com.

Tips, Tools and Tactics
to Begin Reframing

1. Have you been in a personal or professional situation where you snapped? What did that look like?

2. What are some of your fears in relation to a situation that stretches you?

3. Does your team allow a safe environment to express fears?

chapter six

Time to Absorb and Plan

I am probably the biggest Trader Joe's fan … ever. Yep.
I love this grocery store. I even started the fan page for
my local Trader Joe's. If you don't have one nearby,
I'm sorry. Besides the fun-loving, service-minded crew,
flowers in the bathroom and amazing array of foods –
from organic produce to the best dark chocolate ever –
Trader Joe's also has cool sponges. You read that right.
They're not your average kitchen sponges but these odd,
flat sponges. They come 10 to a package, which is the
same size as a package of graham crackers. Actually, they
sort of look like graham crackers. They are that flat.

When you first release a flat, dry sponge from the
package, you can't help but wonder, "How is this going
to work?" Once you run it under water, it's magical. How
can you not feel like a kid when the dry, cracker-like
sponge springs to life and more than quadruples in size?

Absorption makes the sponge grow to its full working potential. Retention such as this also allows us to grow to our full, resilient potential.

Similarly, during the reframing stage, we must take time to absorb our situation to grow into it. Remember, we are trying not to snap. To keep things in perspective, to really embrace your disruption, you'll need to absorb all related nuances.

With my daughter's diagnosis, I got a big dose of absorbing. I had no idea what special-needs children need, and I did not understand the world of therapy. Merritt started physical therapy, occupational therapy, music therapy and hearing therapy. My home had a revolving door of therapists visiting weekly. I was overwhelmed by the extra activity. It hit me one night when the hearing therapist showed up at dinnertime. She could only do evening hours. I looked at my other children, who had suffered a bit because of the many distractions. I decided that Merritt really didn't need hearing therapy during the dinner hour, or ever. I had absorbed a little too much. Metaphorically dripping, I asked the therapist to check back with us in six months. That activity had to be squeezed out to save my sanity.

When you're trying to absorb your disruption, it's important not to take on all of the issues surrounding it. That includes how others process.

It took me about a year to get the balance right. I had to honor what I needed to learn, how to implement these activities and what to relinquish. When absorbing your situation, it might take a few weeks, months or a year. Use that time to absorb what you need to become resilient. Stretch your knowledge, skills and emotions to the point where you feel empowered, not to the point of snapping.

Growing Disruption With Sophia

Not all disruptions swoop in quickly. Some are slow growing and take time to absorb. Sophia Cui was one of the first 25 software engineers at Uber. When she joined the company, there were about 100 employees.

A lot of firsts happened for young professional Sophia at Uber. She worked on interesting problems, ranging from dynamic pricing and dispatching algorithms to mapping and navigation systems to freight and trucking. Sophia said, "Working at Uber, every first happens at an extreme scale." The company was growing at an exponential rate. In the five years that Sophia was at Uber, it grew from 100 to 13,000 employees. Sophia found herself managing 20 engineers despite having very little managerial experience.

The climate and workload were exhausting. Uber is aware of the daunting, daily push-pull. That's why they offer any employee who has been with them for four years as much as a six-month sabbatical. Sophia took those six months. During this pause, she read, cooked and rock climbed, "generally taking time to breathe and regain autonomy."

When we're in a stressful situation, we forget to breathe. But the pauses of life allow us to begin to absorb all that we are going through. In that reflection, we get to choose what to squeeze out and what will fill us up.

By the end of Sophia's six-month sabbatical, she knew she wasn't ready to return to work. "Since graduation, I had lived in San Francisco for seven years working at startups, never taking an extended break. Life has a funny way of leading you down a path that you never planned for. Decisions and priorities get made based on conveniences of the moment. Those small decisions and shifts end up compounding and taking on a life of their own." Sophia and her partner, Preston, began planning another six months of international travel.

After that big trip, Sophia realized, "Burnout takes a long time to recognize and even longer to recover from." Sophia took time to absorb all that had stretched her at Uber. In the end, she realized going back into that environment wasn't the best choice professionally.

While absorbing your disruption, it is perfectly OK to take time off. Slow down and absorb what you've just gone through. This will give you clarity for the next steps.

Tips, Tools and Tactics
to Absorb and Plan

1. What are your responsibilities right now? Make two lists – one with your professional responsibilities and the other with personal responsibilities. Only list the big-picture items, those critical to the success of your organization, team or family. I know you probably take the trash out or send emails to your team, but try to keep them at the 10,000-ft. view.

2. What on that list stresses you out? What is too much to deal with? List those items.

3. Think about what event is specifically stretching you. This tactic is long term. Take a month to really complete it well. Get a notebook or make a spreadsheet. Make spaces/rows for 30 days, then make a column for each of these:

   • Tasks that cause you stress

   • Activities you *must* do, even if they cause you stress

   • Tasks that you may be able to give/assign to someone else

   • A stress-reducing activity you did today

   • Tasks you enjoy

Create this tool and put it here, or go to www.KathyParry.com/rubberbandresilience and download a made-for-you form.

After filling in this form for 30 days and taking time to absorb the issues that surround your disruptive event, pay attention to the last three columns. Begin to assign or give away the stressful tasks. Increase the tasks you enjoy.

chapter seven

Reframing –
Get Creative

The first time I saw a Picasso painting in person was in January 1985. Freezing wind whipped off Lake Michigan and pushed us quickly through the doors of the Chicago Art Institute. My college roommates and I were at the museum that long weekend to see the Degas – the lovely soft lines of ballerinas. That was art to me, and it did not disappoint. As an avid ballet student in my youth, the delicate strokes and calming colors were all I needed to see.

As we rounded the corner into a different gallery, the Picassos came into view. My body experienced a whole new sensation. While the Degas were familiar to my senses and evoked calm, the stark colors and bold lines of the artistic disruptor completely changed my day. I didn't just look at the paintings by Picasso; I tried to figure them out. They called for me to question what I saw.

When Picasso first started with cubism – the art form most closely associated with him because it was so innovative – he was mocked … by peers, art critics and the public. Yet he persisted because, well, that's what true artists do. They are in it for the creativity, the expression. My favorite Picasso quote is, "Every act of creation is first an act of destruction."

When you're trying to create a new normal after a disruptive event, you're going to need to get creative. However, we often think we're being creative when we're really just giving a new version of our old style.

If you've worked on any type of team project, you've no doubt … wait for it … BRAINSTORMED. Ugh. Where did this word come from and can we move on from it? If we think about a storm, a big storm, we know that storms destroy. "Brain tornado" should be the new paradigm for creativity. Destroy what's already in your brain and then start thinking about new tactics. As long as those old visions of delicate dancers come to mind, there is no way to create a cubism line of women with three legs. Just ask Picasso.

During the reframing stage, creative thinking is a must to keep you from snapping. All of the possibilities need to be on the table, including ones you never imagined. Where do those new ideas come from? Usually the universe is speaking to you, but you must be open to listening.

Because Merritt's disease was metabolic, it meant her cells did not turn food into energy properly. This all happened at the cellular level. When I heard this, it took some time to absorb, but then I knew I had to get creative. I did a ton of research. It took me six months to get a certification in plant-based nutrition. I then knew how to feed her a diet that would more easily convert food into energy. My daughter, who had been sleeping as many as 20 hours a day, woke up. She never got sick, and after that first week when we received her diagnosis, she never spent another night in a hospital.

Here's how the universe began to speak to me. My friends (all middle-aged moms and dads) heard about what I was doing. They started asking me questions. It seems they all wanted more energy, too. About this time, I had fallen into a good routine with Merritt. I had some caregivers helping. She had surpassed that two-year mark the doctors had predicted. I wanted to help others with my newfound knowledge of cellular nutrition. Luckily, I was afforded more time to go this direction because my other kids were becoming more independent.

With a background in financial training and human resources, I wasn't sure how I could apply my old skills with the new route I'd be taking. I had a passion for food. (I had even minored in food management in college, thinking that someday I might use it. I had such amazing insight in my youth!) I got creative. I listened to my friends' queries. "Kathy, can you help me feel more energetic?" and "I just wish I could lose this weight and feel better," and more commonly, "I wish my kids would eat better. How do you get your kids to do that?"

My first project was an e-book. Remember those? People loved *A 30 Day Roadtrip to a Healthier Family*. They asked for more, so I listened to the universe and stepped way outside my comfort zone with three more books, as well as blogs and recipes.

Some of those early days of my wellness business felt clunky, like strokes in a Picasso. Eventually I would view all those steps taken that created my business as a thing of beauty. Listening was how I was able to become creative after Merritt's ordeal forced me to stretch. Being still and observant, I was able to go beyond my own ideas. The predictable gave way to astonishing creativity and results.

When I think back to my professional days training employees at bank branches on how to use their ATMs and new computer systems, I realize I probably could have returned to that comfortable route. However, I would have been painting delicate dancers and not bold, striking lines.

A few years later, I listened to the universe again. While my wellness business continued to grow, I discovered that I loved corporate wellness the most. Working with organizations to help increase organizational, leadership and personal energy became the newest branch of my business.

Believe me, there is a huge demand for better wellness in the workplace. According to a National Sleep Foundation poll, 74 percent of Americans admit to being tired during the day. An amazing number of those admit to nodding off, using caffeine or feeling less productive while at work. Speaking at the corporate level led to speaking for organizations and associations internationally. The brush strokes were not the ones I initially envisioned, but helping others has given me such beautiful purpose, more than I could have ever imagined.

Crisis to Creativity

Susan Castriota is a creative person. She is a children's book author and illustrator with a successful book series that features beautiful paintings of her dog, Wilson. He visits different spots, such as the White House. As his story is told, a history lesson also unfolds. Susan has been featured on national television shows, her book was featured at Macy's, and she's also a busy mom. Her life was fulfilling on all levels, but sometimes the worst of times make us excel more than we could ever dream. A double dose of tragic events led Susan to the most creative time of her life.

In 2011, Susan was diagnosed with breast cancer. While she was in the midst of chemo and radiation treatments, her husband filed for divorce. As you can imagine, she went through all the reactions: anger, fear and pain. She recovered from cancer and dealt with her divorce, only to realize she would need more income than what her books brought in.

Susan's creative juices were stunted during chemotherapy. Her old world was destroyed. She didn't want to just write children's books. She no longer had the support of a husband. What was her next turn?

Several times during treatment, she heard, "Limit your use of plastics in the microwave." Curious, she did a little research. She found that some studies linked the chemicals in plastic to breast cancer. These chemicals can leach into food when heated in the microwave. This bothered Susan, so she set off to find non-plastic cookware that could be microwaved. Her creative juices began to flow again. Locating glass containers was easy, but finding lids proved difficult. If she did find one, it didn't fit properly or wasn't vented.

When I asked Susan about her creative process, she said, "I didn't have a lot of encouragement. People didn't think I knew what I was talking about." This is often the case when ideas are new. If you're in an organization that is implementing change, you know that not everyone is a cheerleader for new, outrageous plans. But as Susan continued to explain, "I had to push when I heard 'no' and keep moving toward the next thing."

Susan established Cuchina Safe Lid, which sells non-plastic, microwaveable products. It sounds like an odd niche, but Susan's glass, vented, multi-size lids have been featured on television shopping networks QVC and HSN. She creates recipes and videos to help others use the product and has hired a company for fulfillment. Susan also introduced mini-mitt and pot-holder companion products.

Out of misery, she found a purpose. Her stretch became her mission to help others. You can learn more about Susan and her products at www.cuchinasafe.com.

Tips, Tools and Tactics
to Get Creative

1. What limiting thoughts, skills or ideas do you need to destroy to make room for new ones?

2. Do you regularly challenge "group think" in a work setting?

3. Think about 10-year-old you. Who was she/he? What risks would you take? Put 10-year-old you in your current situation. What would she/he tell you?

chapter eight

Reframing –
Build the Muscle

Merritt couldn't build muscle. Even though the therapists worked with her nearly every day, her body didn't have the ability to get stronger. She had no head control, couldn't make any deliberate movement, couldn't roll over or verbally communicate. At five, she was still a baby, but she was healthy and had taken me down roads I never expected. Such unexpected disruptions have the capacity to help you build your own muscles.

Despite her inability to grow stronger, I kept the therapists coming. Tumbling lessons may not have been in her future (like her older sister), but the act of using muscles was important.

I know a lot about the importance of exercise. My father was not only the head of his family-run business, but he also was an athlete. All of my childhood memories include my dad running, playing handball and, of course, soccer. He started playing soccer in high school at a time when most of the country had no clue what it was.

He chose his college because they had a soccer team. When he had to transfer to the University of Akron because of the Korean War, he started a new team there. As the coach of that team for 17 years, he led them to 118 victories, 43 losses and four ties. His teams won nine Ohio College Soccer Association titles and went to the NCAA playoffs four times.

During my youth, I heard my father say, "Get involved in a team sport." Or "Why don't you go for a run?" The importance of athletics was huge, but so was watching sports … especially soccer. We went to a lot of soccer games.

Imagine how I felt while watching world-class soccer star David Beckham go down on the field with an injury during a World Cup playoff game in 2010. I knew he was really hurt because he had to be carted off the field. I later learned that he had torn his Achilles tendon. Ugh. I knew this was an awful injury that was difficult to heal. In 2016, it all became very clear to me when I, too, went down with a torn Achilles tendon. My injury was not nearly as sexy as David Beckham's; I tripped over a rock near a dark firepit.

My world was disrupted for a while. I had surgery, was on crutches for four weeks and then got a prescription for physical therapy. I was more afraid of physical therapy than the surgery. I knew that building my leg muscles back would not be easy. The therapist presented me with a resistance band, which is really just another form of a rubber band. These giant elastic strips help build muscle as the resistance creates tension. I didn't love it. In all the times I've talked about physical therapy in my keynotes and sessions, no one has EVER jumped up and said they love physical therapy. It hurts.

To build the muscle, however, we need to embrace the resistance.

Ron Builds a Muscle

I met Ron Garrow early in my professional life. We both worked as trainers for a super-regional bank in the South. Everyone loved Ron. He was humble, honest, diligent and kind. He also had a great sense of humor. We would throw paper airplanes into his cubicle or hide his jacket right before a big meeting with the boss. Ron always met such shenanigans with his signature smile.

I left that position and moved back North, but Ron stayed on. He became the head of training and development. A few years later, he moved on to an even larger financial institution and led their training and development. This is where he got his big break to move into an executive human resources role. Ron had always made great career moves and left no ill will behind.

After only a couple of years in this role, he was demoted. Well, he felt like it was a demotion. The organization was hurting in training and development due to a very large merger. No one in the training area had the skills or knowledge to handle a project as large as the one they were facing. Merging another bank and bringing all of their people on board was projected to take a couple of years. Ron was asked to go back and lead the merger.

He told me, "I was angry and started to doubt my own abilities." But Ron was good at training and development. After the initial shock, he got onboard and led the merger initiative. He wasn't happy about leaving the executive position he had waited for so long, but he later reflected on the importance of this part of his professional journey.

"Everything in my professional career had always gone exactly the way I wanted it to. I would grow in one position and leave it to go to a better one, but always without burning bridges." What Ron really wanted next was a chief human resource officer position. After he led the merger, he did what he has always done: He left that company in good standing. He found his next role as that C-suite executive in New York City. Ron told me, "I realized I never could have made that move to the next level if I hadn't had the setback. I had never built a muscle for that type of event. And without that experience, I wouldn't have been prepared for my next role."

Tips, Tools and Tactics to Build the Muscle

1. What muscle do you need to build? What are your professional weaknesses?

2. What would it take to build that muscle? More education? Focus on mental health?

3. Are you taking steps to ensure that members on your team are growing in their career abilities? How?

4. Schedule a time to help your team see weaknesses, both as a team and individually. Devote time to help your team build the muscles needed to become stronger.

chapter nine

Re-energize Definition

The final stage of becoming more rubber-band resilient is re-energizing. Disruptions suck a lot of energy out of us. Both our organizational and personal energy suffer. The good stuff comes, however, after reacting to the disruption and then reframing your mindset. Yes, that's right. If you've maneuvered the first two steps well, you can arrive at a really cool place. Re-energizing gets you back, even better than you were before the disruption.

I've used the analogy of the stretched rubber band to illustrate how a disruption influences our situation. But what's a rubber band designed to do (when it doesn't involve shooting it at someone or something)? The basic use for a rubber band is to hold stuff together. (You'll learn more about the history of the rubber band later.) Can your crisis hold you together? Of course it can, if you allow it to. If you take the next steps toward resilience, you may find the event that left you devastated may also have the potential to create amazing holding properties in your life.

When Merritt was first diagnosed, I had no clue that 17 years later I would be energized by her life. Yes, I know it's ironic that I am energized by a child who has no energy, but the disruption of her diagnosis led me to my current career as a professional speaker. It may be an odd career choice, and one that not a lot of people understand, but it is the way I'm re-energized.

I always delivered my corporate wellness program with telling my "why." Merritt is my "why." While trying to figure out how to best feed my daughter, I did what any mother would do: I turned to Google. Although I minored in food management, tucking those nutrition courses back in the crevices of my brain, I knew I needed more education. One of the best programs available was by T. Colin Campbell, author of the *China Study*. I took an online eCornell certification program offered by Cornell University. Having a greater understanding of how to keep my daughter alive gave me some control over her situation. (What I learned about nutrition and the best way to eat for energy makes up the content of my first book, *The Ultimate Recipe for an Energetic Life*, which is available on Amazon.) So, the story of Merritt's disease and the knowledge I gained about the most healthful way to eat was integral to my corporate wellness programs.

After delivering my presentations, a long line usually

forms beyond the allotted Q&A period. When people have a recognized food authority in the room, they will wait for answers to their questions about quinoa, magnesium or gut health. A woman named Beth was at the end of the line, and her body language told me she was ready for a long conversation. (Attendees who want the longer conversation always go to the end of the line!)

In the early years of my speaking career, I spoke mostly about living an energetic life. Feeling vibrant and well was my passion. This was expressed through cooking demos, two books on eating well and tons of corporate wellness programs. At one of these sessions, I met Beth, an attendee who watched her life transform as she adopted my suggestions.

As the line dwindled, Beth stepped up to talk to me. She held a copy of my book. "Kathy, you may not remember me, but I came to the session you did for us last year." As much as I wanted to say that I remembered her, I was blank.

She continued, "You may not recognize me. I lost 40 pounds this year."

"That's awesome!" I replied. "How did you do it?"

"I was in your session last year and was skeptical before I came. I had tried a lot of things, but I didn't really understand that it wasn't just about what I ate. The story about your daughter inspired me. I bought your book and read your newsletters. YOU helped me transform my health. My high-sugar number came down, and I have so much more energy. I came today to thank you."

The Beths of the world hold me together. They re-energize me and help me realize that my disruption, my beautiful daughter who changed my life, was the impetus for helping people and inspiring me.

Your disruption can be the beginning of greatness.

That's right. After you react and reframe, you can use this thing – the thing that at one point you hated, cried about, stressed over – to become great! You can become great at helping others, great at gaining education, great at starting a movement, great at developing a new talent, great at building better relationships. Your greatness is around the corner. It just takes a few steps to get there.

Alliance Rubber Company

When William Spencer gathered defective inner tubes from the Goodyear Tire and Rubber Company's plant floor in 1923, he didn't know he was on his way to greatness. William thought there might be a use for these discarded scraps. While watching his neighbor's newspaper blow across the front lawn, an idea formed. Maybe these rubber scraps could be fastened into a band to hold the papers together. This was the humble beginning of the Alliance Rubber Company, started by William Spencer in Akron, Ohio.

Today the company is run by Bonnie Spencer Swayze in Arkansas. I use rubber-band analogies throughout my book and keynotes, so I had to learn more about my hometown company that was now run by a woman.

Alliance employs 175 workers and is described by Bonnie as a "culture of family of families." When she talks about her employees, pride and warmth wash over her description. The organization received the state's highest honors because of their generous benefits, which outpace 350 other manufacturers. Employees are eligible for bonuses semi-annually based on profit and as awards for innovative ideas.

When I asked Bonnie about resilience, her upbeat tone changed ever so slightly. As an employer so dedicated to her "family of families," she admitted that the high cost of labor sets her company up to lose money when competing with foreign entities. Alliance Rubber pays their manufacturing employees at least $19 an hour plus another 30 percent in additional benefits. Thailand pays its workers $1.50 an hour.

"So, what do you do to re-energize when you realize the competition is always going to beat you on price?" I asked. "We got aggressive with marketing and innovation," she replied. Alliance offers awards for innovations and makes it easy for anyone in the company to submit new product ideas. They also increased their product line and improved quality. Bonnie listed at least 10 additional ways the company added value for their customers and innovated their products.

When she took a breath after passionately describing their product line, she said, "And the people keep me going. I keep a giant poster over my desk that says, 'Do More of What Makes You Happy.' We let the stress of every day burn us out, but I have fantastic people and I'm dedicated to them. That energizes me."

To learn more about the Alliance Rubber Company, visit www.rubberband.com. You will learn so much about the company and the many uses for rubber bands!

Tips, Tools and Tactics to Begin Re-energizing

1. Do you feel a lack of energy? In which areas – organizational, leadership or personal?

2. If you lead a team, do you have team members who deplete others' energy?

3. What could you do within that team structure to build energy levels?

4. What are some "great" things you can imagine that could happen now?

chapter ten

Steps to Re-energize –
Find Something to Control

"She needs to meet with a physical therapist, and here is the ophthalmologist you need to see for vision diagnostics. Schedule your next appointment with us for three weeks and we'll do some blood work and check her levels. After that, we'll get you scheduled with the specialist in Atlanta."

I left the pediatric neurologist's office completely overwhelmed. Every aspect of my daughter's disease was dictated by others. As a mom of four children under the age of seven, I became used to some degree of daily chaos, but I prided myself on being able to control most aspects of my family's existence. (Every kid left the house with two shoes each, and I even packed lunches every day!) Merritt's disease and subsequent treatment, however, had been usurped by others. I felt powerless.

After about six months, just about the time Merritt was introduced to solid foods, I realized that no medical professional had any advice on how to feed her. Wait. Her cells don't turn food into energy properly, yet no one in that world-class medical facility provided input on what I should feed her? (In defense of the medical community, they've made amazing progress in connecting all the dots between food and health since Merritt's first diagnosis.) At the time, I had to rely on my own background in food and nutrition. It was time for me to take control of something!

As I consulted with holistic nutritionists across the country and tried a cartload of supplements, green super foods and even live algae, I saw my sleepy daughter wake up. She had been sleeping more than the cat, but she soon started staying awake longer. She seemed more engaged. Merritt also hasn't been hospitalized since, which I credit to her new diet. I did that. I controlled that.

When I mentioned my approach to the doctors, they said, "Just keep doing that. We don't study nutrition, and it seems like it is working for her." I controlled a big piece of her treatment. Nobody could take that away from me … or her.

When a crisis happens, we often feel like others are in total control, which isn't fun for most of us, both personally and professionally. When a friend was told that half of her division would move to Dallas, the lifelong Chicago resident felt like she had no choice but to leave the company she'd been with for more than 15 years. She worked through the anger and started to reframe the situation. She started to re-energize when she met with the career counselors provided by the organization. She told me, "When I began to think of all the options in front of me, I sort of started feeling like the kid in the candy shop. I had enough severance pay to take time to work on a certification that I'd been ignoring. But I also considered a complete career change." When she began to control the situation, she re-energized.

The tricky part in re-energizing and finding control during your disruptions is discovering what candy you want to choose. Is it more education? Do you need to hire a mentor or coach? Do you get to address your mental health with a professional? Maybe it's a cross-country move or the end of a relationship.

Whatever your next step, find that one thing you can control and begin taking steps toward grabbing it. Sprinkle it over your disruption and re-energize with your new control.

Raise a Glass to Resilience

After nearly every natural disaster, news crews show up in the aftermath of floods, tornadoes or fires to shoot video of visibly shaken and emotional victims who no longer have homes. Natural disasters happen and no one is ever prepared. We have no control whatsoever over these events. Maybe more so than after any other crises, we want to help because we know it could have been us.

California resident Ken Grossman felt the same way after the Camp Fire swept through Chico, California, in the fall of 2018. Eighty-six people lost their lives, 13,000 homes were destroyed and more than 156,000 acres burned. Ken, like everyone else who survived, had no control over the devastation. He did know one thing he could control: his beer.

Ken, founder and CEO of Sierra Nevada Brewing Company, and his team were greatly impacted by the fire. Fifty of his employees lost their homes. Ken still had his business, which was one thing he could control, so he opened his brewery and restaurant to victims and firefighters.

He then took it a step further. He brewed a special beer, aptly called Resilience Butte County Proud. He decided to donate all proceeds from Resilience beer to fire victims. Ken also thought about his tribe – all the other craft-beer makers. He shared his recipe so other breweries, too, could produce the beer and share profits with fire victims.

Ken told USA Today, "Initially, I was hoping for 200 breweries to sign up, and in pretty short order we had many, many more. When we were at 500, I thought that was pretty amazing. Maybe we could get to 600 or 700." By the time of this writing, more than 1,500 breweries have made Resilience ale and raised more than $15 million.

Recognizing the one thing he controlled – beer – Ken was able to lead a resilient effort out of tragic events, creating camaraderie that sparked a positive outcome for thousands.

Tips, Tools and Tactics
to Begin Taking Control

1. What activities are you always good at? List several.
   If this is a team exercise, list everyone's strengths.

2. How could you use just one of your strengths to create
   a more positive transition?

3. If you're going through a disruption now, what piece
   could you have more control over?

chapter eleven

Steps to Re-energize –
Get Your Tribe Together

Twitter didn't exist. My cell phone didn't take pictures. I had never even heard of posting a dinner picture on Instagram. In 2001, we just didn't have the means to connect the way we do now. Social media, texting and online platforms make it easy to find people. Maybe, if you're lucky, you'll even find your tribe.

What's a tribe? According to the dictionary, a tribe is *a social division in a traditional society consisting of families or communities linked by social, economic, religious, or blood ties, with a common culture.* When I was facing the biggest disruption of my life, I didn't have a tribe of moms who had children with degenerative diseases. The common culture I experienced in my mom tribe was bonding over issues with children who could all walk and talk and go to school. No one in my tribe knew how to hold a child during a seizure or cried at night thinking about their child dying. (Yeah, it was that bad.)

Rudimentary chat rooms of the early 2000s became my savior. I found a tribe. Wow! A few searches on a parent website yielded people who understood me. They knew the anxiety experienced in a doctor's waiting room, woke up at 3 a.m. to see if a child was still breathing, or understood the strain that a special child can put on a marriage. My new tribe member, Amber, knew.

I met her in a chat room for parents of children with diseases like Merritt's. We had so much in common that it was crazy. We both had four children with the youngest being affected by a mitochondrial disease. Our children were all about the same age. We both had a child named Graham. What??!! I had found my *compadre* in the tribe. We corresponded daily, even though we lived on opposite sides of the country.

Our conversations could be as simple as, "What did you give your kids for breakfast today?" to "We just got results from a swallow test back. Do you have time to talk?"

My newfound tribe understood what I faced more intimately than anyone else because they faced it, too. Maybe their child's situation wasn't as severe as Merritt's, or maybe their child was older, or maybe they were a single parent. It didn't matter. They understood parts of my struggle and I could relate to theirs. We were linked by a common culture.

Unfortunately, we sometimes go to the wrong people for support. Most of us turn to family for our biggest support, which is the obvious place to start. We live with some of them, others raised us, or they shared a bedroom with us when we were kids. Sure, that works, but the problem with using your family as your tribe can be summed up in one word: objectivity. Or lack thereof.

Objectivity, or the lack of emotion in response to your problem, is difficult for family members. Family and close friends are best at empathy and sympathy. You need those qualities earlier in your disruption. When you're reacting, call those sisters and brothers, mothers and fathers. You need that. When it's time to re-energize, go to your tribe.

We tend to think our tribe lives at our office or place of employment, but that isn't always the best, either. The people you work with have some of the same issues as your family does. They know too much about a situation to be completely objective. Also, both family tribes and work tribes participate in something that doesn't re-energize anyone: gossip. Step away from the gossip and build your objective, supportive and honest tribe.

But how do you find your tribe? You can start with social media, but we've become shallow in those interactions. When facing professional issues, you can turn to professional organizations you belong to.

You can start by going to a meeting or conference and talking to interesting people. How do you get to the next level? Let people know you're struggling. Vulnerability is definitely a way to create a tribe. People do want to help people. But if you never admit how you're feeling or where you feel weak, no one can step in and be supportive. You must be prepared to give, too. Tribes do that: They look out for each other.

My tribe doesn't always revolve around my daughter. Instead, when I was struggling in my business, I had to find a whole other support tribe. I was trying to figure out how to become a professional speaker, so I attended a free market strategy session sponsored by a firm that sells search engine optimization services. While I couldn't afford their $20,000 SEO package, I did find Renee, a kindred spirit. She had recently quit her job as a nurse educator and was branching out on her own, too. Simply taking a few minutes to talk to her and learn about how her struggles were similar to my struggles led to an amazing friendship and eventually a tribe. We now have five in our tribe of professional speakers who meet and support each other in immeasurable ways.

I look forward to the meetings with this tribe. We sit around a kitchen table for about two to three hours every other month. You can feel the power of commonality. We admit our shortcomings, we share our successes, we ask for direction and we laugh. The meeting is usually followed up later that day with one gesture of support. One person, probably the person who was struggling the most, sends an email. It's simple, but generally it's an expression of gratitude to the group. And as the group email circles around, we all admit that we are energized to get to our to-do lists.

A Noteworthy Tribe

I also found a tribe that has a hashtag. After speaking at a human resources conference, it was natural that I wanted to reach out to some of the amazing HR professionals I met. I thought they hung out on LinkedIn. This makes sense, but I was wrong. Steve Browne, the head of human resources for LaRosa's Family Pizzeria at their corporate headquarters in Cincinnati, Ohio, pointed me to his tribe. After my session, Steve said, "What's your Twitter handle?"

"Oh, I don't use Twitter much. You can find me on LinkedIn and Facebook," I replied.

"The HR tribe is on Twitter, Kathy. If you want to hang with us, go to Twitter," he said. "Use #HRTribe to find us."

After spending some time on Twitter, I saw exactly what Steve meant. It was an extremely supportive community of like-minded professionals. Some hold weekly chats. When someone gets stuck, questions are answered. Many, many HR professionals break the tension with silly memes.

When I interviewed Steve about the #HRTribe, I was surprised by what he shared about his tribe. He said the Twitter tribe wasn't the tribe that meant the most to him. This was a friendly group of people who wanted to belong to something and he loved the group, but his real tribe had created a deeper relationship. At a conference several years ago, Steve met a bunch of people with whom he really connected. Because of his disdain for group texts, they decided to create a GroupMe. Seventeen HR professionals have built a tribe based on support, diversity, humor, non-judgment and *daily* conversations. Yep, every day.

Steve's tribe has experienced divorces, deaths of parents and job loss. "We tend not to solve problems. We listen and commiserate. We only solve when someone asks," he said. Through all that, there is always humor. Group members say "good morning" and "good night" every day. "Too many social groups try to set norms and rules. This group doesn't do that," Steve explained.

I've personally witnessed how people are drawn to Steve. He is gregarious and wears wild shirts, is energized by others and claims they hold him together. He told me, "I'm afraid that people who don't have a tribe are miserable every day."

Tips, Tools and Tactics to Build a Tribe

1. What professional and personal groups do you belong to? List them.

2. Who do you identify with in these groups?

3. If you don't have groups, search your area for professional organizations you could join, or find an online group through Google Meetups.

4. Invite at least one person to lunch, coffee or a phone conversation to discuss issues you're facing. Ask them if they would like to form a more structured group and if they know any like-minded people to include.

chapter twelve

Personally Re-energize

The last stage of re-energizing through your disruption in order to be more resilient is personal, as in just yourself – not your crisis, not the other people, not your organization or your boss. This is about you. Are you doing the best you?

The story of my personal disruption after my daughter's diagnosis also includes the end of my 22-year marriage. As if one life crisis wasn't enough, I went through another. Of course, the statistics are out there. Families under the stress of special-needs children experience a higher rate of divorce. I just never thought that would be me. I don't want to share the details of how my marriage ended. I'd rather focus on what it felt like to re-energize.

The stress of four children, running a coaching and speaking business and trying to keep a marriage together had me losing my hair. No joke. The stress was messing with my thyroid, which in turn made my hair thin. I felt old. Even though I ate really well, I was burning out and feeling bad. It was all stress.

Believe it or not, stress was designed to save our lives. If a bear is chasing you, you're going to fight or take flight. My life was the bear. I had met a bear years earlier, but this one wasn't metaphorical.

My then-husband and I were going to camp and backpack in the backcountry of Yosemite National Park. Before embarking on such an endeavor, you must check in with the park rangers. They want to know where people are in the park, just in case a search-and-rescue operation is ever needed! We filled out a card with our itinerary and emergency contact. The ranger looked over the card and said, "That looks good. Check back in here at the end of your trip. If you don't, we will call your emergency contact 24 hours after your stated arrival time." A trickle of uncertainty slipped down my spine. That unease turned into a stream of apprehension when the ranger gave one last parting instruction, "Oh, you also need to rent a bear-proof canister for your food." Bears. I knew there were bears. We had been backpacking all over the West for over a month. We had a pulley system and usually hung our food in a tree. But this ranger seemed more concerned.

"Our bears are smart. They can figure out those pulley systems. You can rent a canister for five dollars," he explained as I nervously imagined smart bears eating our granola.

We set off and had an amazing first 24 hours in the backcountry. We saw vistas, lakes and streams. No other hikers or bears. The second night was another story.

We heard a rustling near our campsite at dusk. As we turned toward the noise, we saw another camper enter our site. This was rare in the backcountry.

"Hey, I saw you pass my site a while ago," the seasoned-looking hiker shared. "I just wanted to warn you that the bears got my food last night."

"What about the bear-proof canister?" I inquired as I started rummaging for some extra PowerBars.

"Yeah, that thing is too bulky. I never bring it," he said.

We sent him on his way with some food and slowly moved about our site until darkness moved us into our tent. Just as I felt myself drift off with visions of waterfalls in my head, my ex-husband whispered, "Is that your snorting?"

"I'm not snorting!"

"Well, be quiet then and listen."

It was unmistakable. Snorting. And breathing. Really heavy breathing.

"I think it's a bear," he stated the obvious. "Let's be quiet so we can see it."

That bear and his breath and his big, lumbering movements were creating a form of stress I had never experienced. My heart was pounding. I started to sweat. The bear seemed to be about a foot from our thin nylon tent. I had no need to "see it."

"AHHHHHHHH!!!" I screamed. We heard the bear run off.

My body in that moment was doing everything it needed to do to keep me alive. My increased heart rate filled my blood with more oxygen to prepare me for fight or flight. The sweat kept me cool. My body, unbeknownst to me, had stopped digesting my dinner. My many hormones – including those that send signals for sleep, sex and anxiety – spiraled.

Two hormones – adrenaline and cortisol – are released during such stressful situations. If that stress lingers, those hormones at extreme levels cause much more serious side effects. Your thyroid can get messed up, your hair can fall out and you can get acne in your 40s. That's how stress physically manifested during my divorce. Not fun.

Watching the hair fill the sink, I realized I had to do something to re-energize. This thing couldn't continue to burn me out. I turned to a holistic naturopath, my medical doctor and a therapist. This triple coverage of physical and mental advice was my way of regaining control.

I resurfaced after about six months of taking time for me, talking to professionals and taking steps to de-stress. My older sister, Heather, was the first to notice the re-energized me. She said, "Oh, my gosh. You sound like you. I'm so glad you're getting you back."

I was a bit startled by that. I didn't think I had changed that much during my crisis, but I had. I didn't laugh as much. I didn't engage with my friends as much. Everything was about my disruption. This self-care led me back to not only better health but also to my more authentic self. I was doing me so much better.

Has your crisis or disruption affected your health? Are you ignoring signs? I work with some pretty stressed-out people. Those seeking to take steps toward less stress and better health usually ask two questions. First, "Can't I just take a pill?" And second, "Is alcohol an OK way to de-stress?" The answer to both questions is YES and NO.

Supplements can help replace some nutrient loss. A melatonin supplement helps you sleep when you're stressed. Vitamin and mineral supplements can help if you've taken up stress-eating and non-nutritious habits like pizza for dinner and donuts for breakfast. Your body was meant to re-energize with whole, real foods. My first book, *The Ultimate Recipe for an Energetic Life,* has a wealth of pertinent information. It is literally chock-full of answers on how to stay energized, eat well and de-stress. You will get a full rundown on what you need to do. You can find it on www.amazon.com.

Secondly, alcohol can help you release stress … temporarily. As a long-term plan of action, however, it isn't going to cut it. That one drink a day for women or two drinks a day for men is shown to help with stress in the short term, but two-thirds of Americans admit to drinking beyond moderation. (Hey, I sure have!) The effects that alcohol has on your body can also turn into stress at a metabolic level. In essence, the alcohol can end up being a stressor!

So, what do you do? How do you personally re-energize? When can you start? Start now, even if you are right smack in the middle of a life-altering event. Your health is your wealth. Begin to identify how you have been neglecting your health – is it diet, sleep or lack of exercise? After you've identified what is lacking, you can make a plan and IMPLEMENT it. For resources to start your personal energy journey, including "10 Tips to Energize your Afternoon," visit www.KathyParry.com/rubberbandresilience.

A Re-energizing Purpose

When I first knew I was going to interview the CEO of the Vitamix Corporation, I had a preconceived notion of how that interview would go. Jodi Berg, great-granddaughter of the company's founder, has been at the helm of the premier food-blender company since 1999. I visited the

Olmsted, Ohio, headquarters just outside of Cleveland.
Around every corner, I saw examples of re-energizing
culture – test labs for cutting-edge, healthy recipes,
outdoor exercise trails and an historic montage on the
walls about Vitamix's role in the health revolution.

I was surprised when Jodi did not want to discuss kale
smoothies and vegan soups. "Jodi," I asked, "What is a
stressful or disruptive event you have faced?" And her
simple answer was, "Every single day is stressful."

I had guessed that she would credit a special elixir
blended in her A3500 blender as key to helping her
get through trying days. Instead, Jodi shared that she
re-energizes by revisiting her personal purpose each
day: helping people discover their best selves. "I wake
up every day to a lot of 'things' that need to be done.
But that doesn't give me energy," she told me. Having
conversations with her team is what gives her fuel. When
she interacts with her team, she says, it feels like "taking
massive doses of vitamins."

"Everyone's energy level has an impact on the
organization," she said. "My job is to help them find
their superpowers and use them to create a better
company." Jodi believes that superpowers can be found
at the intersection of "what you're good at" and "what
gives you energy." There is a downside, she warns.
Activities that rob your energy can be like Superman
and kryptonite. She encourages her team to focus on
activities that energize them and find someone else

who loves the things they don't (their own personal kryptonite). This rings so true with me! Bookkeeping drains me completely, but the bookkeeper I hired loves the numbers.

When I pressed Jodi for a few tips on how she re-energizes when she's unable to act on her superpower, she said, "I walk, look outside or drink tea. I know those three activities will always bring me joy."

Tips, Tools and Tactics
to Personally Re-energize

1. What causes your stress? List both personal and professional stress.

2. How do you act when you are stressed? Do you shut down? Become short-tempered? Look for comfort in food?

3. How do you address stress? Does your mood affect others, including your co-workers?

Take time today to identify ways to alleviate stress, for example:

- **Mindful minutes of meditation** – Sit quietly for one minute and just breathe.

- **Exercise** – Even if it is just 5 minutes, walk a flight of stairs or around the block.

- **Bring pets to work** – Our furry friends have an amazing de-stressing quality, studies show.

4. Are you eating a diet that energizes you or drains you?

Your body creates energy in the mitochondria of the cell. Energizing foods are whole, real foods. That means foods that come from a tree, a bush or are grown in the ground. (Or it is something that ate something from a tree, a bush or in the ground?) Humor aside, re-energizing food does not include Doritos or chicken nuggets. Whole, real, nutrient-dense foods are the key to re-energizing.

Sugary drinks and simple carb foods are the biggest culprits in a low-energy diet.

List what you eat that may be keeping you from feeling your most energetic.

chapter thirteen

What Does This Book Mean to You?

Right now, I am facing another disruption from the rhythm I was able to sustain with Merritt, now 17. It's 3 a.m. and I hear her coughing. She coughs a lot. Six months ago, I met with a pulmonologist and learned more about what to expect. Through determination and my own re-energizing, Merritt has surpassed by 15 years her original life expectancy projection. But she's coughing … a lot.

She has never been able to lift her head or make any actionable movements on her own. This low muscle tone over time has created a scenario where her esophagus collapses with each breath. Her organs have shifted and are pressing on her lungs. She is in respiratory distress.

The pulmonologist did not think we should see other specialists. Instead, he recommended discussing palliative care. This is a reminder that even though I've gone through all the steps in this book to live a resilient life, disruption will come again.

Disruptions, crises, disasters, displacement and inconveniences are always coming. We can anticipate and possibly plan for some. Remember how Pittsburgh floods ruined Dan's business? How about Susan's bout with breast cancer? These events swoop in, knock the air out of us and leave us on the floor.

This book was meant to help you to have the strength to get up off the floor and to understand that you have the power to work through devastating events. Yes, life will stretch you, but you don't have to snap.

Please use the Tips, Tools and Tactics sections of this book. Peeling back the layers of how we react, reframe and re-energize can be time consuming, and the work isn't always fun. But understanding how you interact with others – family, co-workers or friends – leads to more resilient behaviors when disruptions occur.

For additional resources, visit my website (www.kathyparry.com/rubberbandresilience) and download exercises to use in a professional or organizational setting. Team building is generally just another name for communicating well. So, by communicating about resilience, we build more resilient teams.

If you have an organization that really wants to be inspired to stretch without snapping, please reach out to me about my keynote speaking and half- and full-day energizing summits. I would love to listen to your stories and help you build an energized and resilient team. Share with me how you, or your team, have used the resources and stories of resilience. If you need additional inspiration, feel free to reach out to me at kathy@kathyparry.com.

Final Thoughts

If you haven't stretched a rubber band lately or shot it across the room, do that. Nothing is more fun than watching 1,500 adults shoot rubber bands. It's fun to release that potential energy and watch it soar, no matter what your age.

I have custom rubber bands from the Alliance Rubber Company that I share with audiences. In addition to those custom rubber bands that stretch extra far, I also have a stockpile of rubber-band balls – dozens of colorful bands wrapped together to form a ball that bounces. I send these out as promotions or with thank-you gifts to clients.

My son walked into my office one day and picked up one of the rubber-band balls. As he threw it hand-to-hand and then bounced it off the ground, he asked, "How many rubber bands are in the ball?"

"I have no idea," I replied, somewhat distracted.

I realized he took the ball with him as he left the room. I could hear it bouncing off his bedroom wall. His question made me ponder just how many rubber bands were in each ball. Like in life, the number of intertwined, stretch-inducing rubber bands seems endless.

We have no idea how often we will be stretched, how many times a disruption will come to us, either personally or professionally. The message I always thought the rubber band inspired was about stretching without snapping. As I continued to listen to the ball bounce, I picked one up.

Looking over the ball, I realized it needed all these bands bound together to bounce. One single band will just lie on the floor if we drop it. If we keep our disruptions to ourselves, we face the possibility of winding up on the floor, unable to stretch, snap or bounce. If we bind our distractions, interruptions or crisis up with other people's, we now create a new entity, a resilient structure that not only gets up off the floor but bounces. It rebounds in unpredictable patterns, makes us smile and elicits joy. Resilience isn't just about stretching without snapping but doing it with support. Eventually we soar together.

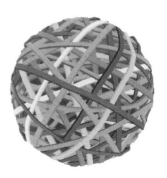

Acknowledgments

Wow, if there is anything I've learned about resilience, it's that you meet a lot of people on the journey. Some people watch you stretch and are ready to catch you if you snap. Some stretch along with you. The most wonderful people on the resilience journey are, of course, the ones who help you bounce. All of these people are part of the rubber-band ball that kept me bouncing!

First, I want to thank the wonderful people who allowed me to tell their stories:

Dan Repischak – Oh, you make me laugh. I'm so glad you can laugh in the face of adversity.

Susan Castriota – Your strength and creativity are beyond inspiring.

Jodi Berg – You have a beautiful spirit and purpose, and the best blender in the world.

Steve Browne – You gather people in and make them feel special. You are the best promoter of others I've ever met.

Sophia Cui – I so respect your perseverance and grit. I can't wait to see what happens next.

Joe Gonzales – Your example of rising above a circumstance is so empowering.

My National Speakers Association family – You are my tribe, and I would not be who I am without you. My Confluence Mastermind, Renee Thompson, Joe Mull, Jeff Tobe, and MJ Callaway, you stretch me and inspire me. David Newman, my coach, you are never boring and are so full of wisdom.

Many, many thanks to Melissa Farr of Back Porch Creative for the amazing layout and design of this book, to Kathleen Green of Positively Proofed for editing, and to Matt Irwin for putting his touch on the first draft.

For my sister Heather, who is no sissy and lived her own resilience journey while I was writing this book. Honey, you are always an inspiration to me.

And those who supported the creation of this book:

- My family, including the one and only Grinch, my father, Stuver Parry.

- My children, Paige, JP, Graham and Merritt, and my bonus children, Samantha, Peyton, Josh and Jackson, for your continued support, laughter and listening to my life lessons.

- My No. 1 fan, Bryan. You stretch me and support me in ways that I never take for granted. We are the true story of resilience, and I love you.

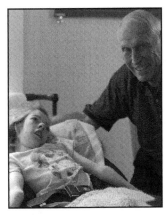

My two big inspirations: Merritt Joy and The Grinch

About Kathy Parry
Corporate Energy Expert

A recognized authority on personal
energy, productivity and resilience,
Kathy Parry ignites positive changes
for professional leaders. Before
launching her speaking and training company, Kathy
was a trainer on a merger-and-acquisition team for a
super-regional bank. In this role, she helped others
integrate new technology and transition through
organizational transformation.

Personal and devastating news about her fourth child
led Kathy to a career where she empowers others to
become more resilient and energized. Kathy works with
Fortune 500 corporate leaders, association leaders and
talent development specialists to help professionals
plan for resilience to positively move through disruptive
circumstances. Attendees leave her sessions with an
action list to power-up their lives and create positive
mindsets toward change.

Kathy holds degrees in Business and Food Management
from Miami University, a certification in plant-based
nutrition from the T. Colin Campbell Program at
eCornell University and a coaching certification from
Wellcoaches. She holds the designation of professional
speaker from the National Speakers Association and

speaks at events nationwide. Kathy has authored three books, is a mother of four and lives in Pittsburgh, where she enjoys a mild dark-chocolate addiction and cooking for hungry friends.

Do you want Kathy to speak at your next conference or meeting? Would you like to tell her your personal story of resilience? Or would you just like to keep in touch and find out what Kathy is eating for dinner? You can reach Kathy at:

www.KathyParry.com
Kathy@KathyParry.com
Twitter: @KParrySpeaker
LinkedIn: KathyParrySpeaker
Facebook: www.facebook.com/KathyParrySpeaker

Would you like Kathy Parry to present at your next conference, leadership meeting or team-building event?

Is your team facing a transitional event? Are productivity or retention levels slipping? Do you want your audience to be super-charged and ready to maneuver disruptions with ease? If you answered "yes" to any of these questions, email Kathy Parry today at **Kathy@KathyParry.com** to schedule a discovery phone call.

Kathy's topics engage audiences and empower them to Get More, Do More, Be More. Using humor, stories and interactive exercises, Kathy delivers keynotes, training sessions and half-day workshops. Participants leave her sessions ready to take action and power-up their lives.

To learn more about programs,
visit **www.KathyParry.com**,
or email Kathy at **Kathy@KathyParry.com**.

Made in the USA
Middletown, DE
15 June 2019